Playtime Devotions

Sharing Bible moments with your baby or toddler

written by CHRISTINE HARDER TANGVALD
illustrated by TAMARA SCHMITZ

Standard Publishing
Cincinnati, Ohio

© 2002 Christine Harder Tangvald. © 2002 Standard Publishing, Cincinnati, Ohio.
A division of Standex International Corporation. All rights reserved. Sprout logo is a
trademark of Standard Publishing. Printed in Italy. Design: Robert Glover.
ISBN 0-7847-1361-8

09   08   07   06   05   04   03   02   10 9 8 7 6 5 4 3 2

Scripture taken from the HOLY BIBLE, NEW INTERNATIONAL READER'S VERSION™. Copyright © 1995, 1996, 1998
by International Bible Society. Used by permission of Zondervan Publishing House. All rights reserved.

Heritage Builders® is a registered trademark of Heritage Builders Association.
Focus on the Family® is a registered trademark of Focus on the Family.

Using Playtime Devotions

In Deuteronomy 6, God instructs us to love Him, to keep His commands, and to teach our children about Him throughout our daily activities. And with *Playtime Devotions,* you can do it!

It's never too early to begin passing on your faith to your child. Your baby CAN learn. Recent scientific research has provided new insights about how children learn as newborns and into the toddler years. *Playtime Devotions* are especially formatted to fit your baby's learning styles at each stage of growth from birth and onward.

> ## Everything you need is in this book.
>
> - Stand the book open where you can glance at it easily—on a dresser, table, or the floor.
> - Each devotion begins with a "key thought": a truth about God that children under four are ready to learn and understand.
> - A short Bible verse comes next, followed by either a game to play, a rhyme to say and act out with motions, or a song to sing. These elements are labeled and have simple instructions highlighted in *italic* type to help you.
> - Finally, cuddle up and pray together. Use the prayer printed with each devotion, or add to the printed prayer to personalize it for your child.

If your baby is a newborn, say or sing each devotion out loud as you rock, feed, bathe, and dress your baby. Newborns learn when their parents speak to them in a high-pitched, sing-song style that is sometimes called "Parentese."

Speaking in this manner, with your face very close to your newborn's, will help his eyes focus on you. The rhythm and rhyme in *Playtime Devotions* will stimulate your baby's brain, help him tune in to the message you're giving him, and help him begin to associate your love with God's love.

Around the age of two months, your baby is beginning to develop basic motor skills. She's practicing moving her arms and legs, getting better and better as she learns more about her hands and feet and what they can do. Helping your baby do the motions that accompany each devotion will help her practice these all-important motor skills as well as add meaning to the lessons you're teaching.

By twelve months, your baby begins forming the sounds he hears you make into his first words. What will those first words be? Now he's ready to sing and rhyme along with you as you go through each devotion. Keep repeating the devotions again and again over time to help him remember what he has learned.

If your style is to have a devotion time in place each day, that's great. If it's more your style to spontaneously use the parts of one devotion at various times throughout the day, that's OK, too. The important thing is to *do* them, and God will bless you for it.

> Each generation can set its hope anew on God; remembering his miracles and obeying his commands. From Psalm 78:7

Bible Verse

God is love.
1 John 4:8

Game to Play

Play peek-a-boo with these words.

**Peek-a-boo
Peek-a-boo
God above . . .**

**Peek-a-boo
Peek-a-boo
Gives us love!**

**Peek-a-boo
Peek-a-boo
I love you!**

**Peek-a-boo
Peek-a-boo
God does, too.**

Prayer to Say

Dear God,
Thank You for Your love. Your love makes me glad!
Amen.

Bible Verse

I will be with you everywhere.
Joshua 1:9

Game to Play

Play patty-cake with these words.

**Patty-cake
Patty-cake
"Hi, hi, hi!"**

**Patty-cake
Patty-cake
"Bye, bye, bye!"**

**Patty-cake
Patty-cake
Now I see**

**Patty-cake
Patty-cake
God's with me!**

Prayer to Say

Dear God,
When I am coming ("Hi, hi, hi!") and when I am going ("Bye, bye, bye!") You are always with me. That makes me feel safe and happy! Amen.

Key Thought — God Is With Me Everywhere

Bible Verse

If I go up to the heavens, you are there.
Psalm 139:8

Rhyme to Say

Say and do this action rhyme.

**If I'm high up in
the air,** *Arms up high.*
**If I'm deep down
in the sea,** *Bend way down.*
If I go anywhere, *Walk in a circle.*
**God always goes
with me!** *Hands out at sides.*

**In the morning sunshine
bright,** *Hands high, round.*
**In the dark when
I can't see,** *Hands over eyes.*
Anytime or anyplace, *Walk in circle.*
God always goes with me! *Hands out at sides.*

Prayer to Say

Dear God,
You never, ever leave me. Never! Ever! I'm glad that
wherever I go, You are always there, too. Amen.

Key Thought: God Made the Whole World

Bible Verse

God created the heavens and the earth.
Genesis 1:1

Game to Play

Play patty-cake with these words.

**Patty-cake
Patty-cake
Arms up high!**

**Patty-cake
Patty-cake
See God's sky!**

**Patty-cake
Patty-cake
The sky's so blue.**

**Patty-cake
Patty-cake
God loves you.**
Give yourself a hug!

Prayer to Say

Dear God,
Thank You for the whole wide world! Your world is special, God. Amen.

Key Thought **God Made Everything**

Bible Verse

You created all things.
Revelation 4:11

Rhyme to Say

Say and do this action rhyme.

**The stars and moon that twinkle at night,
The big round sun that shines so bright –
God made them all!** *Arms up high.*

**The food I eat, the clothes I wear,
My hat, my coat, my underwear –
God made them all!** *Arms up high.*

**The flowers around our big green tree,
Our home and my nice family –
God made them all!** *Arms up high.*

Prayer to Say

Thank You, God, for making everything . . . exactly right! Amen.

Bible Verse

How you made me is amazing and wonderful.
Psalm 139:14

Rhyme to Say

Say and do this action rhyme.

I look in the mirror
Point to eyes.
And I see, see, see
A happy face –
Point to self.
Oh! It's me, me, me!

I look in the mirror
Point to eyes.
And I see, see, see
God made me –
Hands up high.
Just how He wants me
to be!

Prayer to Say

Dear God,
Thank You for making me exactly the way You want me to be! Amen.

Key Thought: God Made All of Me

Bible Verse

God created man in his own likeness.
Genesis 1:27

Rhyme to Say

Say and do this action rhyme.

**Head, shoulders,
  knees, and toes,**
Point to each.
**Eyes, ears, mouth,
  and nose,
God gave me
  all of those!**
Arms up high.
**Head, shoulders,
  knees, and toes.**

Prayer to Say

Dear God,
Thank You for all the parts of me. Head and
shoulders, knees and toes, thank You, God, for all
of those! Amen.

Key Thought
God Loves Me

Bible Verse

We love because he loved us first.
1 John 4:19

Song to Sing

Sing to the tune of "London Bridge."

I love God. Yes, I do.
Shake head yes.
Yes, I do. Yes, I do.
I love God. Yes, I do.
And God loves me!
Point to self.

God loves me.
  Yes, He does.
Shake head, yes.
Yes, He does.
  Yes, He does.
God loves me.
  Yes, He does.
And I love God!
Point up to God.

Prayer to Say

Dear God,
I love You, and I know You love me! WOW, God!
We love each other! Isn't that great? Amen.

God Is So Good to Me

 Bible Verse

The Lord is good.
Psalm 100:5

 Game to Play

Play patty-cake with these words.

**Patty-cake
Patty-cake
Thank You, God,**

**Patty-cake
Patty-cake
For our food.**

**Patty-cake
Patty-cake
Thank You, God,**

**Patty-cake
Patty-cake
You are good.**

 **Prayer to Say**

Dear God,
Thank You for giving us the food we need!
Yum, yum, YUM! You are good to me. Amen.

Key Thought God Cares When I Hurt

Bible Verse

Turn all your worries over to him.
1 Peter 5:7

Game to Play

Play patty-cake with these words.

**Patty-cake
Patty-cake
Play awhile.**

**Patty-cake
Patty-cake
See me smile!**

**Patty-cake
Patty-cake
1, 2, 3.**

**How many teeth
Do I see?**

Prayer to Say

Dear God,
Sometimes my tooth hurts. Ouch! Please help my tooth feel all better—right now, God. Thank You. Amen.

Talking to God Is Important

Bible Verse

Lord, I pray to you.
Psalm 69:13

Game to Play

Play patty-cake with these words.

**Patty-cake
Patty-cake
Say "good night."**

**Patty-cake
Patty-cake
Sleep so tight.**

**Patty-cake
Patty-cake
Watch me pray.**

**Thank you
Thank you
For this day.**

Prayer to Say

Tuck me in, God, nice and tight.
Please watch over me through the night. Amen.

Key Thought I Can Pray to God

Bible Verse

Always pray.
Luke 18:1

Song to Sing

Sing to the tune of "This Is the Way."

This is the way we fold
   our hands *Fold hands.*
Fold our hands
Fold our hands
This is the way we fold
   our hands
When we pray to God!

Verse 2
This is the way we bow
   our head . . . *Bow head.*

Verse 3
This is the way we say
   "Amen!" . . . *Say "Amen."*

Prayer to Say

Dear God,
I know how to pray to You! I fold my hands, and bow
my head, and say, "I love You!" Amen.

God Listens and Cares

Key Thought

 Bible Verse

He cares about you.
1 Peter 5:7

 Rhyme to Say

Say and do this action rhyme.

See my five fingers here. *Wiggle fingers on left hand.*
See my five fingers there. *Wiggle fingers on right hand.*
I fold them like this, *Fold hands.*
And say my prayer!

Whenever I pray, God hears what I say!

See my five fingers here. *Wiggle fingers on left hand.*
See my five fingers there. *Wiggle fingers on right hand.*
I fold them like this, *Fold hands.*
And say my prayer!

And when I talk to God, He does care!

 **Prayer to Say**

Hi, God! It's me! I like talking to You, God.
I'm SO GLAD You listen to my prayers. Amen.

Key Thought: The Bible Is God's Word

Bible Verse

Every word of God is perfect.
Proverbs 30:5

Game to Play

Play patty-cake with these words.

Patty-cake
Patty-cake
I have heard

Patty-cake
Patty-cake
That God's Word

Patty-cake
Patty-cake
Is so true

Patty-cake
Patty-cake
For me and you!

Prayer to Say

Oh, God! Your word is so GOOD and so TRUE.
So for the Bible, I say "Thanks" to You! Amen.

Read the Bible Every Day

Bible Verse

Let Christ's word live in you.
Colossians 3:16

Song to Sing

Sing to the tune of "This Old Man."

Every day, on my way,
I will read God's book
   and say,
That the Bible shows me
   what to do.
And it says, "God loves
   me, too!"

Every day, on my way,
I will read God's book
   and say,
That the Bible shows
   what God can do.
And it says, "God loves
   me, too!"

Prayer to Say

Dear God,
I am so glad we can read Your Bible every day!
It helps me to know what to do. Amen.

God's Word Is Good

 Bible Verse

I have hidden your word in my heart.
Psalm 119:11

 Song to Sing

Sing to the tune of "When the Saints Go Marching In."

Oh, in God's Word
March and clap.
Oh, in God's Word
Oh, in God's Word
 we find Good News!
We find the story of
 God's people.
Oh, in God's Word we find Good News!

Oh, in God's Word
Oh, in God's Word
Oh, in God's Word we find Good News!
We find that Jesus is our Savior.
Oh, in God's Word we find Good News!

 Prayer to Say

Dear God,
Thank You for Your Word. Thank You for the Bible.
I love to read about Jesus in the Bible! Amen.

Bible Verse

Nothing at all can ever separate us from God's love. *Romans 8:39*

Song to Sing

Sing to tune of "Clementine."

**In the Bible
In the Bible
In the Bible I can see
Jesus loves me.
Yes, He loves me.
Jesus loves both you
   and me.**

**In the Bible
In the Bible
In the Bible hear Him say,
That He loves me.
Yes, He loves me.
Jesus loves me every day!**

Prayer to Say

Dear God,
I'm SO GLAD Your Bible tells me about Your Son,
Jesus and His love for me! Amen.

Bible Verse

Keep looking to Jesus.
Hebrews 12:2

Song to Sing

Sing to the tune of "Where Is Thumbkin."

Start with both hands behind back.

Where is Jesus?
Where is Jesus?

Here I am! *Bring left hand out, pointing finger up.*
Here I am! *Bring right hand out, pointing finger up.*

I love you, dear, this morning.
Bow left pointing finger in rhythm.
I love you, dear, this morning.
Bow right pointing finger in rhythm.

Yes, I do! *Hide left hand behind back.*
Yes, I do! *Hide right hand behind back.*

Repeat the song, substituting in different times of the day such as noontime, playtime, bedtime, etc.

Prayer to Say

Jesus, You are always with me. Thank You for loving me all the time. I love You, too—I really do! Amen.

Key Thought: Jesus Is My Friend

Bible Verse

Trust in the Lord.
Proverbs 3:5

Song to Sing

Sing to the tune of "God Is So Good."

**Who is my friend?
Who is my friend?
Who is my friend?
It is Jesus, God's Son!**

**I trust in Him.
I trust in Him.
I trust in Him.
He is Jesus, God's Son!**

Prayer to Say

Dear God,
Thank You for being my friend. It is so good to be able to trust You, Jesus. Amen.

Jesus Watches Over Me

Bible Verse

Jesus said, "Let the little children come to me." Matthew 19:14

Game to Play

Play patty-cake with these words.

**Patty-cake
Patty-cake
Jesus' little lamb,**

**Patty-cake
Patty-cake
That's what I am!**

**Patty-cake
Patty-cake
1, 2, 3.**

**Patty-cake
Patty-cake
Jesus loves me!**

Prayer to Say

Dear God,
I love Jesus. Thank You, God, for Your Son, Jesus!
Amen.

I Love Jesus

Bible Verse

Love the Lord your God.
Matthew 22:37

Rhyme to Say

Say and do this action rhyme.

Jesus, Jesus, I love You!
Clap hands.
**And I know You love
me, too.**
Hug self.

**I want You to be
my friend,
And give me love
that has no end.**

**Jesus, Jesus, it's so true.
Jesus, Jesus, I love You!**
Clap hands.

Prayer to Say

Dear Jesus,
Thank You for being my friend. Thank You for Your love that has no end. I love You, Jesus! Amen.

Key Thought Jesus Is Our Friend

Bible Verse

A friend loves at all times.
Proverbs 17:17

Song to Sing

Sing to the tune of "London Bridge."

Jesus is a friend to me
Point to self.
Friend to me
Friend to me.
Jesus is a friend to me –
A good friend just for me!

I can be a good friend, too
Point to partner.
Good friend, too
Good friend, too.
I can be a good friend, too –
A good friend just for you!

Prayer to Say

Dear Jesus,
You and I are best friends, right, Jesus? I can be a good friend, too. I like having lots of good friends! Amen.

We Love Each Other

Bible Verse

Love one another.
John 13:34

Game to Play

Play patty-cake with these words.

**Patty-cake
Patty-cake
I love you!**

**Patty-cake
Patty-cake
Yes, I do!**

**Patty-cake
Patty-cake
1, 2, 3.**

**Patty-cake
Patty-cake
Do you love me?**

Prayer to Say

Dear God,
Jesus said, "Love one another." Guess what!
We DO! Amen.

Key Thought: Sharing Makes Jesus Happy

 Bible Verse
Share with others.
Hebrews 13:16

 Song to Sing

Sing to the tune of "This Is the Way."

This is the way I share my
 toys
Share my toys
Share my toys.
This is the way I share
 my toys with all the girls
 and boys!

Jesus is happy when
 I share
When I share
When I share.
Jesus is happy when I share
 with all the girls and boys!

 Prayer to Say
Dear God,
I will share because I want to make Jesus happy.
Sharing with others makes me feel happy, too! Amen.

Key Thought | I Can Share

 Bible Verse

Give to people in need.
Ephesians 4:28

 Rhyme to Say

Say and do this action rhyme.

This little boy has two trucks.
Hold up two fingers on one hand.

This little boy has none.
Show other hand as an empty fist.

If this little boy shares his trucks,
Move two hands together; hold up one finger on each.

Then both little boys have one!

 **Prayer to Say**

Dear God,
Help me to share and care for other people . . .
like You do! Amen.

Key Thought: I'm Big Enough to Share

Bible Verse

Be willing to share.
1 Timothy 6:18

Song to Sing

Sing to the tune of "Row, Row, Row Your Boat."

I will share at home.
  I will share at home.
I am big enough to share.
  Yes, I will share at home.

I will share with friends.
  I will share with friends.
I am big enough to share.
  Yes, I will share with friends.

I will share my toys.
  I will share my toys.
I am big enough to share.
  Yes, I will share my toys.

Prayer to Say

Dear God,
Thank You for helping me share. Amen.

Bible Verse

Children, obey your parents.
Ephesians 6:1

Rhyme to Say

Say and do this action rhyme.

If Mommy says, "No!" *Shake head no.*
I don't go!
'Cause Mommy knows what's best! *Arms up high.*

If Daddy says, "Stay!" *Shake head yes.*
I say, "OK!"
'Cause Daddy knows what's best! *Arms up high.*

If Mommy says, "Up!" *Reach up.*
Or Daddy says, "Down!" *Reach down.*
I do what they say *Shake finger.*
And I never frown. *Shake head no.*

'Cause Mommy and Daddy know what's best for me! *Arms up high.*

Prayer to Say

Dear God,
Thank You for my mommy. Thank You for my daddy. I do what they say. Mommy and daddy know what's best . . . because they listen to You! Amen.

Church Is a Happy Place

Bible Verse

Give him glory in the church.
Ephesians 3:21

Song to Sing

Sing to the tune of "Mary Had a Little Lamb."

**My church is a happy
place, happy place,
happy place!
My church is a happy
place.
I like to come to church.**

**My church is where we
learn with friends, learn
with friends, learn with
friends.
My church is where we
learn with friends.
We learn about God's love.**

Prayer to Say

Dear God,
Going to church makes me feel happy inside,
because our church is a happy, happy place!
Thank You for our nice church. Amen.

Key Thought: Go to Church

Bible Verse

We share life with one another.
I John 1:7

Song to Sing

Sing to the tune of "This Is the Way."

This is the way we go to church
Go to church
Go to church.
This is the way we go to church . . . on a Sunday morning!

Verse 2
This is the way we praise the Lord . . .

Verse 3
This is the way we sing to God . . .

Prayer to Say

Dear God,
I like all the people at my church. And I like all the things we learn about You, God, at my church.
Thank You for my church. Amen.

Key Thought: **Praise God Every Day**

Bible Verse

He is my God. I will praise him.
Exodus 15:2

Song to Sing

Sing to the tune of "Clementine."

Let us praise God.
Hands high in air.
Let us praise God.
Let us praise God every day!

Yes, I praise Him,
Always praise Him,
Every day, in every way!

verse 2
Let us thank God . . .
Hands folded in prayer.

verse 3
Let us love God . . .
Hands crossed on chest.

Prayer to Say

Dear God,
I praise You, and thank You, and love You every day.
Amen.

Extra Rhymes & Games

I like my Bible

This is my Bible;
Palms held together.
I'll open it wide
Open hands; keep them touching.
**And say what is written
 on the inside!**
Say Bible words together.

God is near

God is near when the sun shines bright.
Raise arms above head to form sun.
God takes care of me all through the night.
Rest cheek against hands.
God is with me when I play.
Pretend to push toy truck or rock doll.
God is with me every day!
Clap hands.

Mealtime Blessing

Sing to the tune of "POP! Goes the Weasel."
**All around the table we sing
With father and with mother.
We thank You, God, for food and for drink—
and for each other!**

Extra Rhymes & Games

Here Is Jesus!

Sing to the tune of "Are You Sleeping?"
Here is Jesus; here is Jesus.
Point to picture of Jesus.
He loves me; He loves me.
Point to picture, then to self.
Jesus is good; Jesus is happy.
Clap hands.
He loves me; He loves me.
Point to self.

I Love Jesus

Sing to the tune of "Jesus Loves Me."
"I love Jesus," I can say;
  I will love Him ev'ry day!
While I work and while I play,
  I will love Him ev'ry day!

Jesus is alive I know,
  for the Bible tells me so.
He is with me ev'ry day,
  and He hears me when I pray.

Welcome to the Family!

Heritage Builders

Helping You Build a Family of Faith

We hope you've enjoyed this book. Heritage Builders was founded in 1995 by three fathers with a passion for the next generation. As a new ministry of Focus on the Family, Heritage Builders strives to equip, train, and motivate parents to become intentional about building a strong spiritual heritage.

It's quite a challenge for busy parents to find ways to build a spiritual foundation for their families—especially in a way they enjoy and understand. Through activities and participation, children can learn biblical truth in a way they can understand, enjoy—and *remember*.

Passing along a heritage of Christian faith to your family is a parent's highest calling. Heritage Builders' goal is to encourage and empower you in this great mission with practical resources and inspiring ideas that really work—and help your children develop a lasting love for God.

***

How To Reach Us

For more information, visit our Heritage Builders Web site! Log on to **www.heritagebuilders.com** to discover new resources, sample activities, and ideas to help you pass on a spiritual heritage.
To request any of these resources, simply call Focus on the Family at 1-800-A-FAMILY (1-800-232-6459) or in Canada, call 1-800-661-9800.
Or send your request to Focus on the Family, Colorado Springs, CO 80995.
In Canada, write Focus on the Family, P.O. Box 9800, Stn. Terminal, Vancouver, B.C. V6B 4G3.

To learn more about Focus on the Family or to find out if there is an associate office in your country, please visit www.family.org.

We'd love to hear from you!

Try These Heritage Builders Resources!

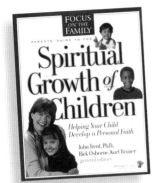

Parents' Guide to the Spiritual Growth of Children

Building a foundation of faith in your children can be easy—and fun!—with help from the *Parents' Guide to the Spiritual Growth of Children.* Through simple and practical advice, this comprehensive guide shows you how to build a spiritual training plan for your family, and it explains what to teach your children at different ages.

The Singing Bible

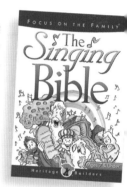

Children ages 2 to 7 will love *The Singing Bible*, which sets the Bible to music with over 50 original, sing-along songs! *The Singing Bible* walks your child through the Old and New Testament Scripture. Introduce Adam and Eve in the Garden, the Ten Commandments, Jonah and the Whale, the Lord's Prayer, and many other biblical characters and facts in this four-cassette collection of songs that will have kids singing along! Memorable lyrics, tongue twisters, and an energetic narrator to guide them make understanding the Bible an exciting journey. Fun and fast-paced, *The Singing Bible* is perfect for listening and learning!

Bedtime Blessings

Strengthen the precious bond between you, your child and God by making *Bedtime Blessings* a special part of your evenings together. From best-selling author John Trent, Ph.D., this book is filled with stories, activities, and blessing prayers to help you practice the biblical model of "blessing." Designed for use with children ages 7 and under, *Bedtime Blessings* will help affirm the great love and value you and God have for your child, and will help each of your evenings together be filled with cherished moments in loving company.

Jesus Loves You

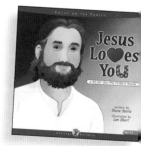

Build your child's confidence in Jesus' constant love and make story time a special family time. Rebus pictures and rhyming text enable your child to be part of the reading experience—and soon he or she will be "reading" to you! Brief questions and Scripture verses offer even more ways for parent and child to interact and further assure your child of Jesus' love.

Heritage Builders
Helping You Build a Family of Faith